101

small WAYS TO

CHANGE THE WORLD

AUBRE ANDRUS

CONTENTS

THINK BIG BUT START

SMALL!

It's hard to believe that one kid could change one habit that eventually changes the world, but it's true! All big ideas start with just one person who decided to do things differently. You could be that person.

Here are just a few ways that small changes can make a big difference…

If everyone on Earth planted one tree, we'd have 7 billion more trees to help absorb carbon dioxide. (Carbon dioxide is one of the greenhouse gases that traps heat in our atmosphere and makes our planet too warm.)

If everyone in America recycled just one aluminum can, 295 million new aluminum cans could be made.

If you shortened your shower by three minutes, you could save 15 gallons of water every day.

See? All it takes is a small action, a minor tweak in habits, or just a little bit of effort. Kids can make a big difference. So start flipping through these pages to discover the many ways you can help!

You can read this book from cover to cover, open it up to a random page, or turn to the checklist on page 108. The important thing is that you start somewhere—anywhere!

Remember to always ask an adult for permission before trying one of these activities. It's important to stay safe when you're out saving the world!

Get your friends or family involved. The ideas in this book will make a difference, but they'll make an even bigger difference when you share them with everyone you know!

Sometimes tackling a big problem can be overwhelming. Stay positive and don't get discouraged. Just remember: every little bit helps.

CARING FOR OTHERS

Look around you! Your life is filled with family and friends who could all use a helping hand once in a while. Not only will you make someone else feel great, but you'll also feel great in return.

HELP AT SCHOOL

Here's some homework for you: try at least one of these ideas for helping friends, teachers, and classmates during the school day.

1 SMILE!

A smile is the universal symbol of kindness. When you smile, it actually makes you feel good even if you've been feeling down. And have you ever noticed that it's contagious? Try it! Smile at someone in the hallway and see what happens.

2 TALK TO A NEW KID

Being new is hard. The next time there's a new kid in your class, there's a quick and easy way you can make them feel welcome: introduce yourself! Try one of these simple phrases and presto—you'll have made someone's day.

Do you like soccer? We need another player.

HI!

HEY!

Hey, do you want to sit with us?

I haven't seen you before. Did you just move here?

HELLO!

3 WRITE A THANK YOU NOTE

Imagine all the people it takes to make a school run smoothly each day: teachers, librarians, lunch staff, recess supervisors, crossing guards, janitors, and more. Wow! Wouldn't it be nice to give them a thank you note to recognize all they do? Here are some things you can write in a thank you note:

I wanted to say thank you for all that you do to make our school great.

You make every school day even better.

Our school wouldn't be the same without you!

The students at our school couldn't get by without your help!

4 TUTOR A CLASSMATE

Do you get perfect scores in math? Always know the answer in history? Or are you known for your great writing skills? If you're good at a subject, offer some help to a classmate who's struggling. Or volunteer to help a student in a lower grade. Your teacher may be able to help you arrange this.

STAND UP TO A BULLY

5

Bullying is not cool. If you're being bullied, or if you see a friend or classmate being bullied, don't let it continue—step up and stop it. Here are some tips you can use when faced with a bully.

ASK FOR HELP!

If you ever feel unsafe around a bully, immediately ask a teacher or an adult for help.

STEP 1

Speak confidently and look the bully directly in the eye. Say something like:

That's not funny, it's mean.

Friends don't treat each other that way.

Stop that now.

WHAT IS BULLYING?

Bullying is mean-spirited. If anyone tries to boss you around, make you feel embarrassed, or harm you, it could be considered bullying. That includes verbal attacks like threats, lies, and teasing, or physical attacks like pushing you or breaking something you own.

STEP 2

Walk away and ask an adult for help. Tell a teacher, librarian, or counselor what happened. Listen for their advice on what to do next.

AM I A BULLY?

Bullying isn't always so obvious. Sometimes small acts or little comments can make others feel bad, like purposely not inviting a friend to a birthday party or saying that you think chess is nerdy to someone who plays chess.

6 SPREAD KINDNESS

What's the opposite of bullying? Kindness. Of course you're kind to your best friends, but it's important to consider everyone's feelings, from strangers to classmates. Not everyone has the same likes, dislikes, hobbies, looks, or abilities, but it doesn't mean that they don't deserve kindness.

Here are some ways you can show kindness at school.

☑ Think about how you would feel if you were in someone else's shoes. Would you feel bad, sad, or mad? Then maybe it's time to make a change.

☑ Be kind even when others aren't. Show your classmates that kindness is cool!

☑ Be inclusive, not exclusive. Include everyone when possible.

☒ Don't whisper or tell secrets about other people.

7 VOLUNTEER YOUR TIME

Teachers are really busy during the school day, and so are other staff members, like librarians and the lunch crew. It takes a lot of people to keep your school running like clockwork. Maybe you could make their day a little easier by volunteering your own two hands! Offer to clean plates at lunch, shelve books at the library, or pick up trash during recess.

☑ Give the librarian a hand putting books back on the shelves.

☑ Pick up any trash you see lying around at recess and put it in the trash can.

☑ Pick up and return sports equipment at the end of recess or gym class.

☑ Give out or collect homework assignments.

8 START A CLUB

Is there an after-school club that you would love to join? Other students probably would too. If something you love doesn't exist, start it yourself! Be proactive by talking to your teacher for advice on how to get started. You could even get your friends involved as the founding members.

CHESS

ASTRONOMY

DRAMA

✓ Drama   ✓ Knitting

✓ Board games   ✓ Drawing

✓ Astronomy   ✓ Magic

✓ Chess   ✓ Poetry

HELP FRIENDS

Someone who's there when you need it most. That's what friends are for, right?

9 CHEER UP A FRIEND

Is a friend at home sick or injured? Collect their homework and any books they might need. You can drop off their assignments and fill them in on what they missed in class and on the playground. Or drop off a homemade gift, like a friendship bracelet, and a get well soon card. A smile or a laugh is the greatest gift there is!

10 SHARE A HUG

FREE HUGS!

Hugging is good for everyone! Scientists have found that a good hug can help reduce bad feelings like stress, and it may even lower your chances of catching a cold. So if a friend is feeling down, give 'em a squeeze! It's quick, free, and will make you both feel better.

11 GIVE A COMPLIMENT

Tell a friend exactly what makes them great—just because! You don't need an excuse to remind someone why you think they're awesome. Write them a note or, even better, give them a compliment in person. It will make their day.

> You always make me laugh. I love your sense of humor!

> I love how creative you are.

> You were amazing in the soccer game today.

> Your science project was the best one in the class.

> You're such a great friend. You always cheer me up.

12 CELEBRATE OTHERS' SUCCESSES

It's easy to feel jealous when a friend does something that you wish you could do, like get a perfect grade, score a goal, or go on a fun vacation. But if you push those envious feelings aside and instead feel happy for your friend, you'll find that your mood will lighten. Think about saying things like:

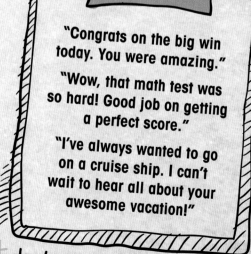

> "Congrats on the big win today. You were amazing."

> "Wow, that math test was so hard! Good job on getting a perfect score."

> "I've always wanted to go on a cruise ship. I can't wait to hear all about your awesome vacation!"

HELP AT HOME

You may not realize it, but it takes a lot of time and effort to make a household run on a daily basis. Chores, bills, dinner, homework—there's so much each family member can do to help.

13 TAKE ON SOME CHORES

Ugh, chores. They're not fun but they have to be done! It's not fair if your parents do all the chores, right? Offer to help your parents tackle some of these boring daily duties like laundry, dirty dishes, garbage duty, and making the beds.

Sit down with your family and create a list of all the chores that need to be done each week. Then assign certain chores to each family member and post the list in a place you can all see it. Teamwork works!

SWEEP SWEEP!

SWEEP THE FLOOR

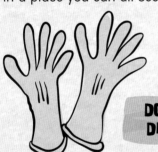

DO THE DISHES

WATER THE GARDEN

14 GIVE AN AWARD

Every family is different, thanks to the unique personalities of each family member. Hold an award ceremony for your family and give out handmade ribbons for all the amazing things each family member does.

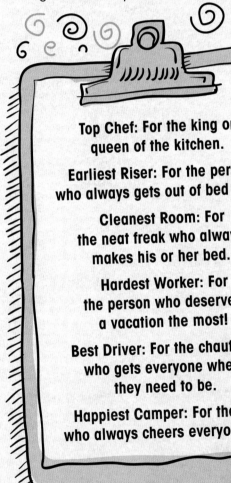

Top Chef: For the king or queen of the kitchen.

Earliest Riser: For the person who always gets out of bed first.

Cleanest Room: For the neat freak who always makes his or her bed.

Hardest Worker: For the person who deserves a vacation the most!

Best Driver: For the chauffeur who gets everyone where they need to be.

Happiest Camper: For the one who always cheers everyone up!

 MAKE IT!

DIRECTIONS

Fold a 12-inch (30cm) piece of ribbon in half and glue it to the bottom of a paper circle. Attach a frill around the edge of the circle by attaching small squares of paper with glue. Using a marker, write the name of the award on the front of the paper circle.

15 SHOW THAT YOU CARE

Your parents spend a lot of time and love making your family great, and a lot of that hard work goes unnoticed. When was the last time you said "thanks!" to your parents? Here are a few ways to make them feel special.

THE GIFT OF GAB

Here's a free gift your parents will love: a conversation! When they ask, "How was school?" don't just say, "Fine." Tell them all about your day—they'd absolutely love to hear about it. And you'll feel better sharing any problems you have or celebrating any great news with them.

A LITTLE TREAT

Give your parents coupons that are redeemable for a chore or a treat! Cut a sheet of construction paper in half, and then in half again. Using a marker, write a message on each coupon with a drawing.

Take a seat. I'll walk the dog this week!

Time for chores? Say no more! I'll be your helper all afternoon. Just tell me what to do!

Forget the shower, here's a full hour! Enjoy an interruption-free bubble bath.

Breakfast in bed? That's what I said! Good for one morning meal from your personal chef—me!

CELEBRATE

A kid's birthday never goes uncelebrated, but what about adults? They don't often make a big deal out of their big day. So why don't you?

Team up with a sibling or another family member to create a list with lots of reasons why you love your parent. For example, "42 reasons why we love you on your 42nd birthday!"

With an adult's help, make a special dinner for your family. Set the table, practice your best manners, and be sure to serve the guest of honor first.

After dinner, serve your parent's favorite dessert—it doesn't have to be a cake! Don't forget to sing "HAPPY BIRTHDAY." And make sure you take care of the cleanup, too!

SAY THANK YOU

Before you go to bed, thank your parents for all the things they did for you today, from making food to driving you to school to helping you study. Let them know that your day was a lot better with them in it.

Create a homemade thank you card, just because. Leave it on your parent's nightstand or in their briefcase. It will be a surprise that surely makes them smile.

THANK YOU!

HELP FURRY FRIENDS

There are millions of pets all over the world that need a home—or just a little love.

16 DONATE TO AN ANIMAL SHELTER

Just as food banks need food and supplies for humans, animal shelters need food and accessories for pets! Check your local animal shelter's website to see what they need most.

COLLAR

WET FOOD

- Wet or dry pet food
- Treats
- Pet beds
- Pet toys
- Cat litter
- Food bowls
- Leashes and collars
- Towels and blankets
- Pet shampoo

PET BED

17 RESCUE A PET

If your parents are willing, adopting or fostering a cat or dog is a better alternative to buying from a breeder or a pet shop.

Adopting a pet means that you'll give a permanent home to an animal that needs one. Animal shelters can only care for pets temporarily, but they hope that every creature will find a new owner as soon as possible.

Fostering a dog or cat means that you'll temporarily provide a home until the pet is adopted by a "forever family." Foster families are really helpful to animal shelters because shelters don't always have the time or space to care for every furry friend. While the pet lives with you, the shelter will help arrange the perfect adoptive parents.

WOOF!

MEOW!

FURTHER READING

If you'd like to get involved, start by checking in with your local animal shelter—sites like petfinder.com can help.

23

EAT LESS MEAT

Some people don't eat meat because of their love for animals. Others don't eat meat because of their love for the environment. But how does what we eat affect Earth?

Raising and feeding animals, like cows and chickens, takes up a lot of land and a lot of water. And making and selling packaged meat creates a lot of greenhouse gas emissions, which add to global warming problems. If we eat less meat, we'll save water and create less pollution.

TRY IT!

Challenge your family to eat less meat each week. Start with "meatless Mondays," where you don't eat meat for breakfast, lunch, or dinner. No bacon, no deli meat, and no burgers—sorry!

WHO DOESN'T EAT MEAT?

- Vegetarians don't eat meat or fish and power up with food like eggs, cheese, vegetables, fruits, and grains.

- Vegans do not eat or use any animal products, not even milk or eggs. Instead they eat vegetables, fruits, and grains.

- Pescatarians don't eat meat, but they do eat fish as well as vegetables, dairy, fruit, and grains.

HELP WILDLIFE THRIVE

There may be 7 billion humans on this planet, but we have other neighbors we need to consider: insects, mammals, plants, and flowers, to name just a few! Here are some ways to support the wildlife in your neighborhood. Ask your parents to consider one of these ideas.

START WITH...

Offer to help water plants or fill the birdseed in a feeder, and your parents may be more willing to let you try one of these ideas!

- **Hang a bird feeder. Birds pollinate flowers, eat insects like mosquitoes, and are fun to watch.**

- **In a garden or window box, try growing some plants and wildflowers that are native to your area. Bees can find nectar, birds can find shelter, and insects can feed on them.**

- **Consider a birdbath or a fountain. It's great for more than just birds—frogs like them too!**

- **Ask to plant a tree in your backyard, in a community park, or at school. Birds can nest in them, caterpillars can grow in them, and deer and other animals can find shade and shelter.**

DONATE

Got stuff? Sure you do! But do you really need it all? Here are some things you can easily part with that can make a big difference to other kids' lives.

20 DONATE YOUR OLD STUFF TO YOUNGER KIDS

Look around your room. Is there a toy, book, stuffed animal, or piece of clothing that you haven't used in more than a year? It might be time to let it go. Instead of letting it sit unused, that item could be used and loved by another kid. Wouldn't that make you feel good?

Donate items to places like Goodwill, the Salvation Army, Toys for Tots, or local organizations that help families in need. These organizations donate or resell your items at a low price.

FREE STUFF!

21 DONATE YOUR PONYTAIL

Do you have long hair? If you have 10–12 inches (25–30cm) to spare, you might be able to donate your hair. Organizations use donated hair to make wigs for kids who suffer from hair loss due to diseases like cancer. It's a win-win situation: you'll get a fresh new look while helping others. You'll feel like a million bucks!

WARNING!

Don't cut your hair at home! Ask an adult to take you to a hair stylist. Put your hair in a ponytail or braid before it gets cut. It will be easier to mail that way.

22 DONATE SPORTS EQUIPMENT

Whether you outgrew your equipment or stopped playing, that unused sports stuff could be put to use by someone else. Donate it to a local school or place of worship, or to an organization that collects equipment for kids in need.

 FURTHER READING

You can donate your hair to:

Locks of Love **locksoflove.org**
Childhood Leukemia Foundation **clf4kids.org**
Children with Hair Loss **childrenwithhairloss.us**
Wigs 4 Kids **wigs4kids.org**

You can donate sports equipment to:

The Sports Shed **thesportsshed.org**
Leveling the Playing Field
levelingtheplayingfield.org
U.S. Soccer Foundation's Passback program
ussoccerfoundation.org/programs/passback

23 DONATE FOOD

Food banks are always in need of healthy boxed and canned goods all year round —not just during the holidays. Check your local food bank's website and you'll often find a wish list of items. Here are some safe bets:

☑ canned fruits and vegetables

☑ brown rice

☑ canned soup

☑ baby formula and food

☑ canned tuna

☑ mixed nuts

☑ spaghetti sauce

☑ dried fruit

☑ dried noodles

☑ powdered milk

☑ dried beans

☑ tea and coffee

ASK AN ADULT!

Ask a parent's permission before raiding your pantry for donations.

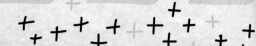

24 HOLD A SALE

Sell something—anything!—then donate the money you make to charity. Friendship bracelets, cookies, and lemonade are easy and affordable ways to raise money for a great cause. Make sure your customers know it's a fundraiser. Tell them about the charity and why you believe in it. And don't forget to say thank you!

Tips for Success:

• **Before you start, make sure you have some smaller bills and coins so you can make change.**

• **Ask a friend to help—one person can sell, and the other can collect the money.**

• **Display the prices and the cause you are supporting clearly with labels and signs.**

• **A colorful tablecloth and eye-catching display can help attract customers.**

👆 FURTHER READING

Find your local food bank at: **feedingamerica.org** or **foodpantries.org**.

Alex's Lemonade Stand Foundation (**alexslemonade.org**) encourages kids to send donations from their own lemonade stands to help find a cure for childhood cancer.

25 ASK FOR DONATIONS INSTEAD OF GIFTS

For your next birthday, or during the holiday season, ask for donations to charities instead of gifts. Pick three causes that you believe in, and share donation information with your friends and family. You may not even notice the lack of gifts—after all, parties are about celebrating with others and you can do that with or without presents.

 FURTHER READING

WHERE SHOULD I DONATE MY MONEY?

These organizations are making a big impact around the world.

Wildlife Conservation Society **wcs.org** seeks to protect wild animals around the world.

Equality Now **equalitynow.org** fights for justice and equality for girls around the world.

The Lunchbox Fund **thelunchboxfund.org** provides daily school lunches to at-risk kids in rural South Africa.

Environmental Defense Fund **edf.org** works to protect the planet from climate change and pollution.

Room to Read **roomtoread.org** helps kids in Africa and Asia learn to read and supports gender equality in schools.

26 DONATE A PORTION OF YOUR ALLOWANCE EVERY MONTH

If you had $10, what would you do with it—spend it, save it, or give it away? How about all three? Practicing not spending all of your money is a good habit to start now. It will make it easier for you to manage your money when you become an adult.

✂ MAKE IT!

YOU WILL NEED

- Three glass jars with lids
- Puffy paint or letter stickers

DIRECTIONS

Using the paint or letter stickers, label each jar with one word: SPEND, SAVE, or GIVE. Each time you receive your allowance or birthday money, divide it among your three jars. For every $10:

40% spend = $4 to use now

40% save = $4 to put aside

20% give = $2 to donate

LEND A HAND

Donating your time and energy is the best way to get personally involved with a cause. You'll see the difference you're making in real time—and you'll feel great doing it.

27 VOLUNTEER

A volunteer is someone who does a job without getting paid. Many organizations can't stay in business without them! Being a volunteer means you're giving your time and skills freely to support a great cause. Your reward is all the warm and fuzzy feelings you'll have while you're making a difference.

IF YOU ARE AN ANIMAL LOVER, VOLUNTEER AT YOUR LOCAL ANIMAL SHELTER

You may be asked to walk dogs, play with cats, refill water bowls, clean up, and give out treats. Each shelter has different rules about how old you need to be, or if an adult needs to accompany you. Just call and ask!

IF YOU'RE A GREAT TEAM PLAYER, VOLUNTEER AT YOUR LOCAL FOOD BANK

Sign your whole family up for a volunteer shift! Food banks need help organizing all of the donations they receive. You may be asked to check expiration dates, sort items, re-package bulk food into smaller portions, or even serve food. You'll have to work together as a team to tackle these tasks quickly and effectively.

IF YOU ARE CREATIVE OR CRAFTY, MAKE AND DONATE ITEMS TO CHARITY

Some charities focus on gathering handmade items such as hats, blankets, scarves, and more. If you're a creative person, invite some friends over and start crafting! Project Linus (www.projectlinus.org) donates handmade blankets to children in need. All blanket styles and sizes, including no-sew fleece blankets, are welcome as long as they are washable.

 FURTHER READING

These sites can help you find a volunteer opportunity in your area:

DoSomething.org

VolunteerMatch.org

YSA.org

IN YOUR COMMUNITY

The world is a big place. But big changes start with small actions—and those actions can start in your own backyard.

28 BE COURTEOUS

Your neighborhood is like a big family. Certain rules keep it running smoothly and keep the people who are a part of it happy. Here are some you can follow:

Trash belongs in trash cans—nowhere else.

Treat your neighbors' yards with respect. It takes a lot of work to cultivate a lawn.

Ever heard of noise pollution? It's above-normal levels of noise that can disturb your neighbors. Be respectful and keep your music and your voice down.

If you see something suspicious, tell an adult straightaway. Neighbors can help protect each other from vandalism and theft, and help keep little kids and pets safe from harm, too.

29 OFFER UP ASSISTANCE

Sometimes next-door neighbors feel like an extension of your family. After all, when you live so close it's easy to keep an eye on each other. Think about the people who live nearest to you. How could you help them? Here are a few ways you may be able to lend a neighborly hand:

A pet owner may want a dog walker or a cat sitter from time to time.

An elderly neighbor may need someone to rake leaves, collect the mail, or mow the lawn.

A younger neighbor may want some help with their homework, or learning a new sport.

30 START A NEIGHBORHOOD LIBRARY

Reading is fun! And it has a lot of other benefits too: it reduces stress, fills your mind with new words and ideas, and helps you focus. Why not bring the love of reading to your neighborhood?

Organize a book swap in your neighborhood. Ask everyone to bring at least one book. Display all of the books and let guests pick one or two to take home.

Little Free Library (littlefreelibrary.org) offers instructions on making your own mini library (it also sells pre-made ones). Place these outside your house near the sidewalk so anyone can swap books.

(31) BE CURIOUS

Your community is just a snapshot of the diverse world you live in. And it's the perfect way to learn more about some of the people and cultures around the globe. Our differences make us interesting!

Do you know of a family in your neighborhood, or a classmate at school, that's different from you? Maybe they are from a different country, speak another language, or celebrate different holidays. Ask them about these things! In addition to all the interesting differences, you may find you have a lot of similarities, too.

32 TAKE A CPR OR FIRST AID CLASS

The skills taught in CPR and first aid classes can help you react quickly and confidently during an emergency. These are skills you can use at school, at home, or in your community! You never know when someone will need your help.

CPR

CPR stands for cardiopulmonary resuscitation, and it can save someone's life if they've stopped breathing. The American Heart Association says children as young as nine can learn CPR.

ASK AN ADULT!

Ask an adult to help you sign up for and attend a class. They might want to take the class too!

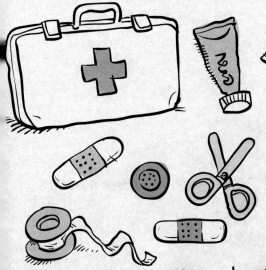

FIRST AID

Babysitting courses from organizations like the Red Cross are a great way to learn basic first aid skills. Classes like these will teach you how to get help during an emergency and also how to deal with minor injuries like bruises, sprains, or cuts.

33 JOIN A SCOUTING PROGRAM

There are Scouting organizations all over the world—and some have been around for more than 100 years. They may have slightly different names, but they all teach important values like teamwork, giving back, and self-confidence. Plus, you'll meet a ton of new friends! Most Scouting programs take kids as young as six right up to adults as old as 25.

Here are some things Scouts get to do:

Try out cool sports like archery, kayaking, or rock climbing

Wear a uniform and decorate it with badges they've earned

Camp and hike in the woods

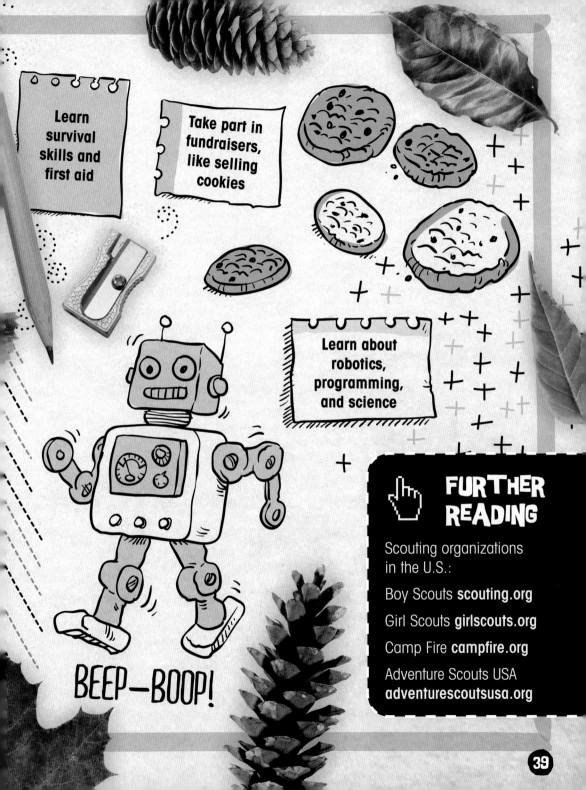

Learn survival skills and first aid

Take part in fundraisers, like selling cookies

Learn about robotics, programming, and science

BEEP–BOOP!

FURTHER READING

Scouting organizations in the U.S.:

Boy Scouts **scouting.org**

Girl Scouts **girlscouts.org**

Camp Fire **campfire.org**

Adventure Scouts USA **adventurescoutsusa.org**

CARING FOR THE PLANET

We're so lucky to live on this beautiful planet. But it needs our love and care. We can all play a part in keeping Earth such an amazing place. Let the following pages inspire you!

SAVE ENERGY

Make these little changes on a daily basis and you'll make a big difference over a lifetime.

34 UNPLUG

BZZZ!

Turn it off and you've saved electricity, right? Wrong. When something is plugged in, electricity is being used—regardless of whether the switch is on or off. In fact, 75% of an appliance's energy usage is when it is turned off. Some people call this "vampire energy."

A phone only needs a few watts of energy to charge. But those watts add up—the average home in the U.S. uses more than 10,000 kilowatts per year! Save electricity by unplugging small appliances when they're not in use.

- ✓ television
- ✓ video game system
- ✓ stereo
- ✓ phone charger
- ✓ laptop charger
- ✓ printer
- ✓ computer
- ✓ coffeemaker

TURN OFF THE LIGHTS

Flick the switch to "off" when you leave a room, and you do a lot more than just reduce your parents' electricity bill—you help save the environment. Reduce energy and you'll reduce pollution. It's as simple as that!

The majority of the electricity we use is created by burning fossil fuels, like coal and gas. But burning fossil fuels creates greenhouse gases and contributes to global warming. When the temperature of our planet increases, sea levels rise, severe weather patterns occur more often, and some plants and animals could become extinct.

👆 FURTHER READING

Find out more about energy at:

U.S. Department of Energy **energy.gov**

Mother Nature Network **mnn.com**

the U.S. Energy Information Administration **eia.gov/kids**

REDUCE POLLUTION

The way we get around each day has a big impact on global warming and pollution. The good news is that there are simple steps you can take—literal steps!—that are much more eco-friendly.

36 THINK TWICE BEFORE GETTING IN THAT CAR

Instead of driving, ask your family to reconsider how they get around each day. There are many other options that are less harmful to the environment.

WALKING

Every time someone in your family drives in a car, they are polluting the environment. But there's one easy way you can break that habit—walk instead! Every step your family takes is a little bit less pollution in our air, and it's great exercise. Sit down with your family and think about how you could adjust your schedule to drive less. Who can walk to school or work? Can any errands be done on foot?

BIKING

Too far to walk? Try riding a bike! If your family can bike to school or work a few days a week, that's great news. If not, ask your family members if they're interested in taking up a new weekend hobby: biking! It's an eco-friendly way to get where you need to go—and it's really fun.

PUBLIC TRANSPORTATION

If you live in a city, buses and trains are an exciting way to get around. And because more people fit on a train or a bus than in a car, a lot less air pollution is produced. The more crowded the bus or train is, the more efficient it is!

RECYCLE

To recycle is to convert waste into reusable material. It makes sense! Why let something sit in a landfill when it can be repurposed into something else?

37 VISIT A RECYCLING PLANT OR LANDFILL

Every day, we create trash. A lot of it. According to the Environmental Protection Agency, one person creates a little more than 4lbs (1.8kg) of trash per day! Do you know what that looks like? Take a trip to a local recycling center or landfill for a free tour and you'll see how all that garbage adds up. Prepare to be shocked.

FACT!

Each year, the world creates more than 1 billion tons of garbage.

FACT!

The U.S., China, and Brazil create the most trash.

FACT!

According to the Environmental Protection Agency, only about 30% of garbage gets recycled—even though a majority of it is recyclable.

FACT!

The largest collection of garbage in the world is in the middle of the Pacific Ocean. The Pacific Garbage Patch is as big as Texas!

FACT!

Landfills create air pollution as well as water pollution, which can contaminate nearby drinking water.

INFORMATION

How long does it really take for garbage to decompose?

Glass = 1 million years

Styrofoam = 500 years

Plastic bottle = 450 years

Disposable diaper = 450 years

Tin can = 50 years

Newspaper = 6 months

Apple core = 2 months

FACT!

The city of San Francisco, California, recycles about 80% of its trash!

RECYCLE PROPERLY

Recycled items like paper, plastic, and aluminum first go to a sorting facility, which separates the items, compresses them, then transports them to be repurposed. It takes a lot of work to make the system run smoothly. Follow these rules and you'll be a big help!

TIP

Rinse out any dirty items before throwing them in the recycling bin. If any food remains, the item may have to be thrown in the trash pile instead.

WHAT CAN I RECYCLE?

Glass: All glass can be recycled, including compact fluorescent light bulbs

Plastic: Milk jugs, water bottles, soda or juice bottles, peanut butter containers, yogurt tubs, cereal box bags, and more

Paper: Newspapers, magazines, junk mail, receipts, greeting cards, paper cups, cardboard boxes, and more

Metal: Aluminum cans, tin foil, bottle caps, and more

GLASS BOTTLE

PAPER CUP

MILK JUG

ALUMINUM CAN

WHAT CAN'T I RECYCLE?

☒ Plastic bags

☒ Dirty paper plates

☒ Greasy pizza boxes

☒ Styrofoam containers

☒ Pet food bags

☒ Waxed or laminated paper

☒ Most juice boxes and milk cartons

GREASY PIZZA BOXES ☒

CHALLENGE!

Challenge your family to reduce the amount of trash they create each day and increase the number of items they recycle.

PLASTIC BAG ☒

39 PICK UP LITTER

Litter is any kind of garbage that is dropped on the ground instead of placed in a trashcan. Cigarette butts, soda cans, plastic bags, and gum wrappers are common pieces of litter.

Invite some friends to help clean up your neighborhood, local park, or beach. All you need is a garbage bag and some rubber gloves, and you can make a big difference. Every piece you pick up helps!

SAFETY FIRST

Always wear gloves when you're emptying trashcans, and never pick up sharp objects, like broken glass and syringes, with your hands.

WHY IS LITTER BAD?

Litter makes our beautiful planet look ugly, and it can also be dangerous. During a storm, litter that's found on sidewalks can be washed down drains and eventually end up in a river or the ocean. This can pollute the water and endanger animals, who might choke or get caught in the trash.

Composting is nature's way of recycling! It transforms decomposed items into nutrient-filled soil, which can then be used to help plants and gardens grow. A compost pile is just that—a pile of compostable items!

To start your own, put some items from the list below in a small section of your backyard. (Make sure to ask an adult if it's OK!) Compost piles should be turned over with a garden shovel every few weeks, and should be kept damp with a garden hose.

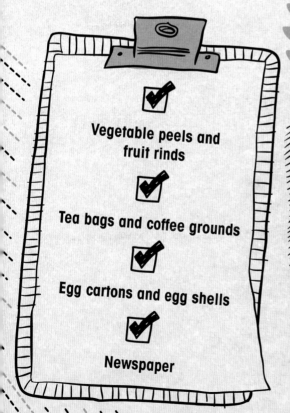

☑ **Vegetable peels and fruit rinds**

☑ **Tea bags and coffee grounds**

☑ **Egg cartons and egg shells**

☑ **Newspaper**

WHAT CAN I COMPOST?

☑ **Paper towel**

☑ **Brown paper bags**

☑ **Dry leaves and grass clippings**

REPURPOSE

One of the ways to reduce waste is to repurpose an item instead of throwing it away. "Repurpose" means to find another use!

41 ## MAKE A HOMEWORK "MAILBOX"

Keep your homework and other important papers organized in this repurposed cereal box. Place it near your bedroom door or the front door, so you don't forget to grab what you need on the way to school.

 ## MAKE IT!

DIRECTIONS

1. Ask an adult to cut the sides of a cereal box diagonally until they reach the center of the box. At the halfway mark on the front of the box, cut straight across.

2. Cover each side of the box by gluing colored paper to it. Or create a collage by overlapping scraps from magazines.

3. Finish decorating your box with stickers, rhinestones, ribbon, or markers

YOU WILL NEED

- Cereal box
- Scissors
- Colored paper
- Glue

CEREAL-LY USEFUL

These containers can also be used to store books, magazines, artwork, and more.

42 CREATE A BOTTLE PLANTER

Plastic soda or water bottles can be transformed into cute plastic pots that are perfect for small indoor plants or cacti. Learn more about these kinds of plants on page 68!

Learn more about these kinds of plants on page 68!

 MAKE IT!

DIRECTIONS

1. Ask an adult to cut the plastic bottle about halfway down.

2. Paint the outside of your pot. Add a face or patterns if you'd like to! Let it dry.

3. Put a layer of pebbles at the bottom of your pot to help with drainage. Then add soil. When your plant is in position, add more soil to hold it in place.

YOU WILL NEED

- Plastic bottle
- Scissors
- Acrylic paint
- Paintbrush
- Soil and pebbles
- Plant

LOTS OF POTS

These pots can also be used as storage for pencils, art supplies, or jewelry.

CRAFT

Before tossing that cardboard or plastic egg carton, find a way to give it a second use. Here are just a few ideas, but we bet you could come up with a ton more!

43 DESIGN A TRINKET ORGANIZER

Open the egg carton and lay it flat in a drawer. Fill the small sections with things like paper clips, rubber bands, and loose change—anything that usually rolls around a junk drawer. The larger section can hold scissors, pencils, and more. Or use it to store craft supplies. Beads, buttons, and more fit perfectly in these little pots.

MAKE AN EGG CARTON GAME

Have you ever played Mancala? It's an ancient game that's been around for centuries—and it's as much fun to play today as it was then.

HOW TO PLAY MANCALA

The aim of this ancient game, based on planting seeds, is to collect the most game pieces—or seeds.

Each player has one row of six cups, and a winnings tray at one end of the board. To start the game, place four game pieces in each of the 12 cups.

The first player picks up all the pieces from any cup on their own row. Moving counter-clockwise, they drop one piece in the next cup along, and so on until the pieces run out. If they reach their own winnings tray, they drop one piece in it. If they reach their opponent's tray, they skip it.

MAKE IT!

DIRECTIONS

1. To make the game board, cut off the top of the egg carton, then cut the top in half.

2. Glue one half to each end of the egg carton to create a tray on both sides. Let it dry.

3. Use your paint or markers to decorate the game board any way you like.

If the last piece is dropped in the player's own winnings tray, they get another turn. If the last piece is dropped in an empty cup in their own row, they win that piece and any pieces in the cup directly opposite. All winnings go into their tray.

Play continues until one player has no pieces left in their row. The other player then puts all their remaining pieces in their tray. Time to count up! Whoever has the most pieces in their tray wins!

REUSE

When you reuse something, it means you're not throwing it away—and that's a good thing!

45 SAY "NO" TO PLASTIC

About 85% of the world's plastic is not recyclable. That means millions of tons of plastic end up in landfills every year. But things are changing. In 2016, France became the first country to ban plastic utensils, plates, and cups! Follow in France's footsteps: instead of going for plastic, pack reusable silverware in your school lunch.

The same goes for water bottles. In America alone, 2.5 million plastic bottles are thrown away every hour. Instead of buying bottled water, carry around a durable reusable bottle. They come in all shapes, sizes, and styles and can easily be filled up at a water fountain or from a filtered water pitcher at home.

46 BRING REUSABLE CONTAINERS TO SCHOOL EACH DAY

The average American creates more than 4lbs (1.8kg) of trash every day. An easy way to help reduce that is to challenge yourself to create a garbage-free lunch.

Taking your lunch to school in a reusable lunch box is a great start. And, if you avoid plastic by using a stainless steel container, this is even better for the environment.

SAY "YES" TO

- ✓ Reusable lunch box
- ✓ Reusable containers
- ✓ Metal silverware
- ✓ Reusable bottles
- ✓ Fabric napkins
- ✓ Bulk snacks

SAY "NO" TO

- ✗ Paper bags
- ✗ Sandwich bags
- ✗ Plastic cutlery
- ✗ Plastic bottles
- ✗ Paper napkins
- ✗ Individually wrapped snacks

47 TAKE CLOTH BAGS TO THE GROCERY STORE

Plastic bags are complicated! They can be recycled—but you can't simply drop them into your regular recycling bin because they cannot be automatically sorted by recycling machines. In fact, they can get caught in the machines and break them.

Plastic bags can only be recycled by a special process, so they have to be dropped off at a special facility—but most people aren't willing to take the time to do that. By using cloth bags, you eliminate the problem! Encourage your family to keep reusable bags in he car and their purse, briefcase, or backpack.

If you've collected a few plastic bags, reuse them as garbage bags for small trashcans, dog waste bags, or shopping bags.

BAGS FOR EVER

When plastic bags end up in a landfill, they can take up to 1,000 years to decompose!

48 BUY USED

Thrift shopping. Used. Secondhand. Whatever you call it, buying something that's been previously owned by someone else can be a great idea. It means you're giving an item a second life instead of letting it end up in the trash. It's also cheaper than buying something new.

☑ Clothes
☑ Shoes
☑ Books
☑ DVDs
☑ Backpacks
☑ Sports equipment
☑ Toys
☑ Bikes

49 REUSE SCHOOL SUPPLIES EACH YEAR

Back to school is an exciting time for everyone! And back-to-school shopping is part of the fun. But do you really need all-new school supplies every year? With a little planning, you can reuse most of your school supplies and buy only what you need. Here are some tips:

Write your name on all your school supplies. That way if you lose anything, it can be returned to you.

At the end of the school year, store your leftover supplies carefully in your backpack. They'll feel like new when you grab your backpack again in a few months!

HAND IT OVER

Garage sales, local secondhand stores, or online resale sites like **craigslist.org** are all great places to find gently used items. Turn to page 26 to learn how you can donate your unwanted stuff to a secondhand store!

During the school year, take care of your belongings. That might mean keeping your pencils in a case and keeping your backpack clean for your folders and notebooks.

REDUCE

Every day, people add a little bit more pollution and garbage to our planet. It's hard not to! But there are so many ways you can cut down on your impact.

50 BUY LOCAL

When you buy something "local" it means that it came from a place near you. It didn't have to travel on a truck, a plane, or a ship to get to you. That happens more than you think! After all, how does a banana that's grown in South America get to a house in the United States? It's traveled thousands of miles from a farm to a grocery store to your front door.

Buying local reduces the amount of pollution that's created from this process. It also helps support local businesses, which is good for your community. Here are some ways your family can buy local:

Buy fruits and vegetables from a farmer's market.

Choose holiday or birthday gifts from a local craft show or boutique.

Eat at a local family-owned diner instead of a big chain restaurant.

Grow your own food! See the gardening tips on pages 70–71.

Shop at a local bakery for bread and cake.

51 BUY THINGS IN BULK

Individually packaged snacks like raisins, crackers, and potato chips are really handy for school lunches. But they can also be wasteful. Think of all the packaging that surrounds the food and how much (often non-recyclable) garbage is created once you've eaten it.

When you buy something "in bulk" it means you are buying a larger portion of the item in a big box or bag. It might cost a little bit less and it often has less wasteful packaging.

Instead of buying individually portioned snacks, you could buy one large bag and place small portions in reusable containers every day. It takes a little bit more time, but you'll have created much less garbage and pollution—and you may have even saved some money.

52 BUY LESS

Think about your favorite store at the mall: every single thing inside it had to be designed, created, and shipped to you. Think about how much energy, water, and other resources it must have taken! And how much pollution was created. By buying less, we reduce our ecological footprint.

One way to buy less is to buy or ask for "experiences" instead of things. Over holidays or birthdays, see if your family would be interested in doing something fun together, like making memories and learning something new, instead of buying a toy that might end up sitting on a shelf.

INFORMATION

WHAT'S AN ECOLOGICAL FOOTPRINT?

Everyone has one—even you! It's the quantity of environmental resources—such as water, food, and electricity—you use each day. We obviously want our "footprint" to be as small as possible.

According to the World Wildlife Fund, globally we are acting as if we have the resources of 1.5 Earths. This means our renewable resources could completely run out in the future. The good news is that making small changes every day can make a big difference!

HOST A SWAP WITH YOUR FRIENDS

53

Have you ever really wanted something that your friend has? Well, maybe they'll trade you for it! Swaps are a really fun way to get "new" stuff without spending any money—and more importantly, it's great for the environment because you're not buying anything new, and you're not throwing anything away.

STEP 1 - PICK A THEME

It might be toys, books, video games, board games, clothes, or movies.

FAIR SHARE

If there are any leftover items at the end, donate them to a charity. Turn to page 26 for some ideas.

STEP 2 - INVITE YOUR FRIENDS

Tell each person that they must bring three items. Everything should be clean and unbroken.

STEP 3 - SET UP A DISPLAY AREA

Make sure there is room for each person to display their items. A cleared-off floor or table is fine.

CHECK FIRST

Be sure to ask your parents for permission before giving your items away.

STEP 4 - START SWAPPING!

Let one guest shop at a time. To "buy" something, just offer one of your items as a trade.

54 BORROW

Another way to reduce your ecological footprint? Borrow instead of buying! Borrowing means you have something temporarily, then other people get to use it. It's a good way to get lots of use out of one item. Here are some tips to get you started:

55 GO DIGITAL

Technology has made it very easy to get rid of "stuff." Not too long ago, every photo had to be printed on paper and stored in a heavy photo album. Now we can just click through thousands of photos online.

But when you go digital, it's about more than just less clutter. It also means fewer physical products need to be made, which means less pollution and garbage. Here are some tips for going digital:

 Check out books from the library.

 Rent sports equipment or musical instruments.

 Borrow a movie or video game from a friend.

 See if your neighbor will lend you a board game.

 Ask a sibling if they'll lend you some clothing.

SCREEN LIMITS

Remember that looking at screens for too long isn't good for your health—set yourself limits and take regular breaks!

E-readers allow you to read digital books instead of paper ones. Music streaming services let you listen without having to buy music!

Instead of paper greeting cards, ask your family to send an e-card over the holidays, or digital invitations for your birthday party.

SAVE PAPER

Trees release oxygen so we can breathe, provide shade that keeps us cool, and help fight climate change. But despite all of these amazing things, billions of trees are cut down every year. What can tree lovers do to help?

56 USE BOTH SIDES OF THE PAPER

It's no secret that lots of trees have to be chopped down to make paper. The process also uses a lot of other resources, like oil, which in turn creates pollution. Instead of using paper carelessly, start to conserve!

Turn used printer paper into scrap paper by cutting it into quarters and writing on the back. Use it for notes or give it to your parents for grocery lists.

Use both sides of your notebook paper. If you write with a pencil, you can erase it later.

Buy recycled paper whenever you can.

Only print when it's absolutely necessary, and use both sides of the paper.

FURTHER READING

DON'T FORGET TO RECYCLE!

According to the American Forest and Paper Association, only about half of the paper we use gets recycled. And just a third of that recycled paper goes on to create new paper. Paper can only be recycled five or six times. Eventually the wood fibers get too weak and have to be mixed with new paper to create a strong sheet.

Still, every time we recycle paper, we are helping to save trees. So it's important to use paper only when you absolutely must, reuse it when you can, and put used paper in the recycling bin.

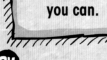

57 PLANT A TREE

About 15 billion trees are cut down each year around the world. Luckily, there is one simple way we can help counteract the effects of deforestation—plant a tree!

There are many places you can plant a tree: your backyard, a neighborhood park, a community garden, or your school. (Always ask for permission before planting anything.) Visit a local nursery or garden center to purchase seedlings or a small tree. An adult can help you safely dig a hole and care for the tree as it grows.

WHAT IS DEFORESTATION?

It's the permanent removal of trees in order for the land to be used for other purposes, like farming, grazing livestock, or building new houses. If deforestation continues at its present rate, all the world's forests could disappear in the next 100 years.

58 USE FEWER PAPER TOWELS AND NAPKINS

Think twice before you grab a napkin! Paper towels are convenient, which means it's really easy—too easy—to reach for one every time we need to clean up a mess or dry our hands.

Cloth towels are a more eco-friendly way to clean up a mess. Ask if you can switch to reusable cloth napkins and recycled paper products at home. And when you're in a public restroom, use the electric hand dryer!

NO WASTE PAPER

Used paper towels and napkins can be composted. Turn to page 51 to learn more about composting.

SAVE WATER

Although water is a renewable resource (which means we won't run out of it), it could become limited in the future. That's because only 3% of the water on Earth is drinkable fresh water, and the population keeps growing.

59 TAKE A SHORTER SHOWER

When it comes to saving water, showers are definitely better than baths. And shorter showers are even better! That's because every minute you shower uses five gallons (23 litres) of water. Think about it: if you take 10 minutes to shower, you use 50 gallons (230 litres) of water. But if you cut your shower down to 7 minutes, you only use 35 gallons (160 litres) of water.

Next time you hop in the shower, set a timer and challenge yourself to take the shortest shower possible while still getting clean. Start a month-long competition with your family by recording each of your shower times. See who used the least water at the end of the month.

60 TURN OFF THE FAUCET

How else can you conserve water? With a simple twist. Never let the water run from the faucet for no reason. Here are some tips to keep in mind when you're helping out with daily chores or taking care of yourself:

Don't let the water run when you're brushing your teeth.

Only run the dishwasher when it's completely full.

There's no need to pre-rinse every dish before putting it in the dishwasher.

Instead of washing dishes one at a time, just fill the sink up with hot water, and use that water to wash all the dishes.

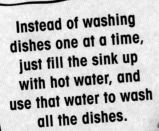

START A MINI POTTED DRY GARDEN

Plants love water, right? Well, not always. Some plants, like succulents and cacti, need very little water. They're really good at storing up water in their thick leaves. These kinds of plants are great for the indoors, as long as you can keep them near a window. They may not need a lot of water, but they do need sun!

SUCCULENT CARE

Succulents like to be watered until the soil is wet, but then shouldn't be watered again until the soil is completely dry. During the winter, they'll need even less water than usual. Ask someone at a garden center or nursery to help you pick out the perfect assortment and soil for your indoor garden.

PLANTS ARE GOOD FOR YOU!

Just like trees, indoor plants release oxygen and absorb carbon dioxide. Even a mini potted garden can make the air in your family's home cleaner. Some even say that plants can make you feel happier!

62 HELP YOUR FAMILY BE "GREEN" WHEN DOING LAUNDRY

Is that dirty laundry pile getting taller and taller? Doing laundry is no fun, but being eco-friendly is! At least you can feel good the next time your family tackles this chore—if you follow these tips.

THE NOSE KNOWS

Before you throw something in the dirty laundry pile, take a sniff: if your clothes don't smell or have any obvious dirt on them, they might not need to be washed, especially if you only wore them for a few hours.

☑ Use cold water when running the washing machine. (Ask your parents before changing any settings.)

☑ Fill the machine up all the way! That means waiting until your laundry hamper is full, or combining your laundry with a sibling or parent's.

☑ Instead of using the dryer, hang your clothes on a drying rack or clothesline.

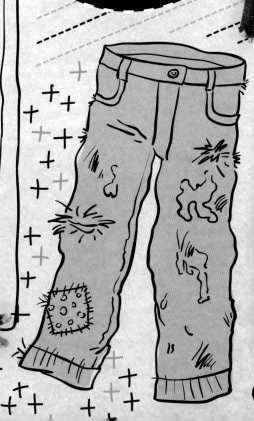

GET INVOLVED

If there is a cause you believe in, like being more friendly to our planet, don't keep your passion to yourself—share it with others!

63 PLANT A GARDEN

Some say getting your hands dirty puts you more in touch with the environment. Give it a try! A garden can teach you how our food is grown as well as how to care for a living thing. Sure, it's not a pet—but a garden needs just as much love. And it's just as much fun to care for! You'll want to get your whole family involved for this project. It's a big deal, but it's so worth the effort.

💡 INFORMATION

WHICH GARDEN IS FOR ME?

Indoor herb garden: Herbs like rosemary, cilantro, or mint can be grown inside or outdoors in small pots. They smell great and can be used by your family for cooking.

Raised-bed garden: Got a big backyard? Then there may be room for a large sectioned-off garden where you can grow all sorts of vegetables, fruits, and herbs, depending on where you live.

Container garden: If you have a small backyard or just a patio, potted plants like tomatoes are a great place to start. Make sure they get a lot of sun and water!

Community garden: Many towns have community gardens where you can rent a small plot of land that's just for you. It's like having a backyard… but it's not quite in your backyard.

☑ Lettuce grows very fast and takes up little space. Your salad will taste even better if you know you grew it yourself.

☑ If you have a big backyard, raspberry bushes are a great addition. There's nothing like eating a fresh raspberry straight from the bush.

☑ Carrots are perfect for raised-bed gardens. They need deep soil to grow well.

☑ Tomatoes are good for garden beginners. There are so many kinds of tomatoes—try a few different ones.

☑ Zucchini grow on vines, so they like lots of space, but they can be grown in large pots too!

☑ Strawberries grow well in the ground or in a pot—even with just a patio, you can grow your own dessert!

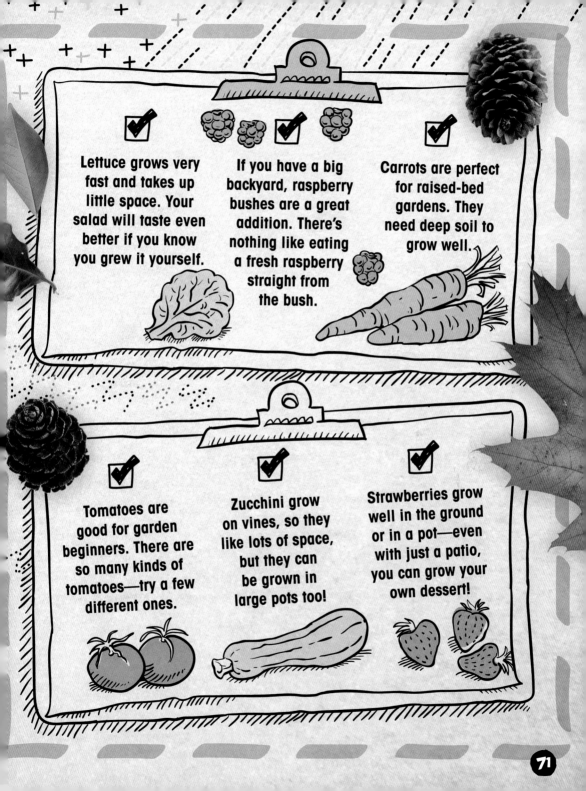

64 SPEAK UP!

If you feel strongly about something, tell the world! Maybe you think your school needs more trees, or your town needs more recycling bins, or the government needs to do a better job of reducing pollution. Here are some ways you can let your voice be heard:

Write a letter or email to your local or national government official. Their contact information can be found on your city or country's official website. (You may even be able to call and talk to them directly!)

Start a petition to bring awareness to an issue, and encourage your community to sign it. Websites like change.org can help you get started.

Join your school's student council or run for class president. Or you can take on a leadership role for a club that you've joined.

Attend a city council meeting or a local rally. Kids can't vote, but you can show support by being present and voicing your opinions.

65 VISIT A NATIONAL PARK

National parks are beautiful, protected spaces that are found all around the world. The plants, animals, and habitats within that area are kept as natural as possible so they can live safely forever. That means things like highways, hotels, homes, and even humans could be banned from certain areas.

When you step inside one of these places, it's hard not to be amazed by its beauty. And nature has a way of making us feel calm and at peace. It's never a bad idea to spend an afternoon or a week-long vacation outdoors with your family.

Entrance fees to these parks help keep the area protected, clean, and safe. So not only do you get to enjoy amazing sights like mountains, volcanoes, caves, waterfalls, and more, but you'll also be supporting environmental protection.

66 EDUCATE OTHERS

Maybe you're passionate about global warming, or becoming a vegetarian, or about adopting animals. You might wonder why others aren't as passionate as you. It could be that they don't know enough about that issue. So why don't you teach them?

Not everyone will share your beliefs and passions, but they might like to learn about important world issues. Here are some tips for starting the conversation:

> Write a report for extra credit at school. Ask your teacher if you can present it to the class.

> Work with your teachers to organize a special event or day at your school, like a Recycling Awareness Day.

> If your school has a newspaper or newsletter, offer to write an article about the topic you care about most.

> Create a blog that teaches others about a topic that might be new to them.

CARING FOR YOURSELF

Don't worry, we didn't forget—we just saved the best for last. It's time to think about Y-O-U. Because looking after yourself is just as important as looking after the planet!

STAND UP FOR YOURSELF

You matter, and so do your thoughts and feelings.
Everyone deserves to feel loved and heard.

67 BE YOUR OWN BIGGEST FAN

It's important to be an advocate for yourself. To "advocate" means to speak in favor of or support. That's right—you need to be the champion of your own self! There are many ways you can do this, and it's not only about speaking up when something is wrong. It's also about having confidence and celebrating your wins.

If you feel scared, say, "I'm not going to do that." Then walk away.

If you're feeling creative, raise your hand and say, "Hey! I have a great idea!"

If you feel like no one is listening, say, "Excuse me. I'd like to say something too."

If you feel excited, say, "I have to tell you all about this!"

If you feel left out, say something like, "I'd like to be a part of this too."

If you feel proud, say, "Look at this! I'm really happy with how it turned out."

68 ASK FOR HELP

You're not a superhero. That means you're not perfect, and that's okay. Instead of bottling up your emotions, let them out! Every now and then, everyone needs a little help—even those people whose lives look perfect on the outside. Everyone feels the same things at one time or another, so you don't need to feel embarrassed about it!

Here are some things you can say when you need a boost:

If you feel confused you could say, "I don't understand. I need that explained again."

If you feel nervous, you could say, "I could use a little confidence boost right now."

If you feel overwhelmed, you could say, "I need a little alone time right now."

If you feel sad, you could say, "I really need some cheering up."

If you feel stumped, you could say, "I really need help figuring this out."

A PROBLEM SHARED

If you ever need to talk to someone, teachers and school counselors are great people to turn to for advice.

If you really need a hug, say, "I need a hug!"

69 SAY YES!

Do you usually shy away from the unknown, or do you jump in feet first? Saying "yes!" is a great way to experience new things. Trying something new is thrilling, and you may be surprised at what you learn about yourself.

Eat something you've never tried before—something you think you don't like. Try at least three bites before making a decision.

Get to know someone who is outside of your friend group—someone you may not have a lot in common with. Once you start talking, you'll probably find some similarities.

Try a sport that you've never played. You may be a gymnast who's secretly really good at basketball. Give it a shot!

Go someplace you've never been, like a park, library, museum, or neighborhood. What did you discover?

Pick a book in a genre that you'd never usually read. For example, grab a mystery even though you usually like comic books.

70 SAY NO!

Saying "yes!" can lead you to a lot of fun experiences, but saying "no" is just as important—especially if you feel uncomfortable. Saying "no" doesn't mean that you are boring or don't know how to have fun—it means that you know yourself. Don't let friends boss you around, and don't feel pressure to follow the crowd. Your happiness is important. Listen to your gut, and don't apologize.

If you don't want to do something, it's okay to walk away from the situation. You could say, "I'm not going to join you," or you could suggest a different idea by saying, "What if we did something else instead?"

If you can't afford to do something, don't feel embarrassed. Just tell your friends that you won't be able to participate. If they ask why, don't feel pressured to tell them more than you feel comfortable sharing. You can always say, "My parents won't let me," or "I already have plans with my family."

If you're asked to do something illegal or dangerous, you could say, "I'm not going to do this, and you shouldn't either." Then walk away and ask an adult for help.

BE POSITIVE

Even when it feels like you'll never escape the stormy weather, there are ways to let the light shine through the clouds.

71 DON'T BEAT YOURSELF UP

Have you ever felt that you failed? That you could have tried harder, been faster, or acted better? You're not the only one—everyone feels this way from time to time. You are often your toughest critic. Hey, you expect the best, and there's nothing wrong with that. But you also need to give yourself a break every now and then. Some days are better than others. That's all. Tomorrow is a new day—remember that!

72 STOP COMPARING YOURSELF WITH OTHERS

There's only one person you should compare yourself with: yourself! Did you do better than yesterday? That's all that matters. Everyone learns and grows at a different rate.

Just because someone else got an A on a test doesn't mean that you should have too. Just because someone hit a home run, it doesn't mean your second base steal wasn't great.

People have different strengths. In most things in life, there will always be someone who is better than you, and someone who is worse. But the only person you should be concerned about is y-o-u. Be happy with where you are today, and be proud of trying your best.

73 LOOK ON THE BRIGHT SIDE

When something doesn't go your way, it's easy to get angry. Fast. But there's a flip side to everything. Instead of choosing to be angry, you could choose to be optimistic. Being optimistic means you can find some good even in the worst situations.

I may have sprained my ankle, but at least I get to cheer on my teammates from the sidelines and help out my coach.

I did not get a good grade on this project, but my teacher promised to give me extra help so I can do better next time.

It's raining outside, but now I get to spend time hanging out with my entire family, which is actually pretty fun.

74 LOVE YOURSELF

Grab a blank sheet of paper and a pencil. You could easily write down three reasons why you love your best friend, right? But what about three things you love about yourself? Think about what makes you unique and why your friends and family enjoy spending time with you.

KIND FUNNY
SMART
FRIENDLY
STRONG
THOUGHTFUL
CREATIVE
BRAVE

75 STAND TALL

Confidence is key! And one easy way to show you are confident is with a power pose. Start with good posture. That means shoulders pulled back, chin up, eyes forward, and a straight back. For an added boost, put your hands on your hips. Now imagine a superhero cape flowing behind you!

Take that power stance in front of a mirror—it makes you looks fearless, right? And here's a secret: even if you're not feeling confident, standing in this pose can make you look confident.

BE KIND, UNWIND

Just because someone is mean to you, it doesn't give you permission to be mean back to them. Tell them to stop, walk away, and ask an adult for help.

76 DON'T HOLD GRUDGES

A grudge means you're still mad at someone, even after they say sorry. If a friend said or did something mean to you—but they really did apologize sincerely—think about forgiving them. You don't want to lose a great friendship over something small. It may have seemed like a big deal at the time, but once the dust settles, you'll probably realize that it's not a big deal after all.

Play with your dog outside.

Shoot some hoops at an outdoor basketball court.

Offer to help your parents garden or rake the leaves.

Play in your backyard with friends.

77 GET OUTSIDE

Did you know that we need the sun to survive? It's true! Without it plants can't grow, we would be shivering from the cold, and we wouldn't have enough Vitamin D. Vitamin D makes our bones strong. Some people even say that sunlight makes us happier. Really! A daily dose of sunshine is just as important as brushing your teeth. Make sure you get outside every day.

Read a book in a park.

Walk or ride your bike to school.

WEATHER WISE

Always wear sunscreen on hot days and don't forget a hat and mittens when it's cold outside.

Eat lunch at a picnic table.

78 DISCONNECT

From TVs to tablets to laptops to phones, kids are spending a lot more time sitting and staring at screens these days. Sure, there are so many fun games, movies, shows, and text messages just waiting for you, but it's really important to take a break from screens every now and then. Not only will it give your eyes a rest, it will also give your mind a rest! Instead of looking at a screen...

Head to the kitchen and try a new recipe for something edible, like chocolate chip cookies, or something fun you can play with, like DIY slime. (Ask an adult for help!)

Pick up a book from the library on magic tricks, crafts, or science experiments.

Take on a puzzle, board game, or Lego project with your entire family.

Try to write a story, a song, a comic, or a poem. Add illustrations too!

POWER DOWN

Ask your parents to turn off the wi-fi for an afternoon, or hand over your devices to them for a full day—or even a weekend!

I tried my best on the spelling test.

Lily said she liked my shirt.

My friends laughed really loud when I told a joke during lunch.

79 CELEBRATE THE LITTLE THINGS

The weather was perfect today.

This is a great dinnertime tradition to start with your family, or something you can practice by yourself before you go to bed: recite at least three great things that happened today. Even the smallest things count!

We got to eat cupcakes for my teacher's birthday.

80 JOIN A SPORTS TEAM

When you're a part of a team, you get to make strong friendships, learn new skills, and practice healthy habits. Guess what? All of those things make you a happier person! Don't restrict yourself to just the sports your friends are a part of. Join a team that excites you. It's important to follow your own interests and dreams. Here are a few ideas you could try…

- ☑ basketball
- ☑ lacrosse
- ☑ gymnastics
- ☑ hockey
- ☑ baseball
- ☑ soccer
- ☑ figure skating
- ☑ horseback riding
- ☑ swimming
- ☑ tennis

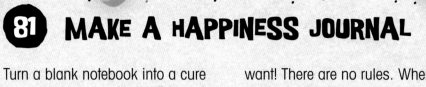

81 MAKE A HAPPINESS JOURNAL

Turn a blank notebook into a cure for a bad day. Inside, list things that make you happy. You could write, draw, scrapbook—whatever you want! There are no rules. Whenever you're feeling down, open it up in search of a smile. Here are some things you can include:

☑ song lyrics you love

☑ happy memories

☑ the people you love most

☑ photos that make you laugh

☑ your favorite places

☑ silly jokes

☑ quotes that make you smile

EAT HEALTHY

Food fuels your body and your mind—the healthier you eat, the healthier your mind and body will be.

82 EAT BREAKFAST

You've heard it before: it's the most important meal of the day! Then why do so many people skip breakfast? It's because mornings are rushed, and people are often running late. But breakfast is so important that it's worth getting up 15 minutes earlier for a filling meal. Here are some quick breakfast recipes that are a great way to start your day...

yogurt with berries, granola, and a drizzle of honey

slice of wheat toast with peanut butter, banana slices, and raisins

English muffin with cheese, fried egg, and a tomato

peanut butter and jelly on toast

bacon, egg, and cheese on toast

scrambled eggs with peppers and cheese, and a side of toast

oatmeal with apples and cinnamon

granola bar, a banana, and a glass of milk

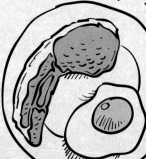

HAVE A HEALTHY SNACK

There are a lot of snacks out there—some are not very healthy, like candy bars and potato chips. Healthy snacks will help you feel full and won't give you a sugar crash. After all, the point of a snack is to make your stomach settle down until your next meal so you can focus on your day. When you're hungry, it's hard to do well in school, and you might get grumpy too. But a healthy snack will boost your brain power—and your mood.

☑ fruit like grapes, apples, or bananas

☑ celery sticks with peanut butter

☑ carrot sticks with hummus

☑ rice cakes with peanut butter

☑ trail mix made with raisins, nuts, and popcorn

84 EAT MORE FRUITS AND VEGGIES

Fruits and veggies—you can't live without them! Kids need about five portions of fruit and veggies per day. But most kids don't eat enough of the healthy stuff, even though it's filled with good things like vitamins and minerals, which keep you healthy and strong.

EAT A RAINBOW

Whenever you eat, try to make your plate as colorful as possible. If your plate is usually filled with white or brown food, you probably aren't eating enough fruits and vegetables.

GIVE IT A TRY!

Ask an adult to help you try a recipe that includes these fruits and veggies.

CARROTS

They really do keep your eyes healthy! Try carrot sticks dipped in hummus.

BROCCOLI

This green vegetable has an extra helping of vitamins and minerals. And it tastes great mixed with eggs or pasta.

BELL PEPPER

These peppers aren't spicy—but they are filled with vitamins. Try them chopped up with eggs or sliced on a sandwich.

CAULIFLOWER

It's not as colorful as the other vegetables, but it is really good for you. Try it mashed up like mashed potatoes. You can barely tell the difference!

ORANGES

Get your Vitamin C fix! Eating the real thing is even better than drinking the juice. Add orange slices to your breakfast or lunch as a side dish.

GRAPES

They keep your blood flowing and your heart pumping, and they're super easy to carry around as a quick snack.

APPLES

Here's another quick snack, and it's good for your brain too. Make sure you eat the skin.

BLUEBERRIES

They may be small, but they are mighty—mightily healthy! Sprinkle these on top of cereal, yogurt, or oatmeal. Or add them to a smoothie.

💡 INFORMATION

NOT A FRUIT OR VEGGIE LOVER?

You don't have to eat them plain or raw. Try them in another form, maybe a soup or a smoothie.

You don't have to eat them alone. Sprinkle fruit on top of yogurt or oatmeal, add vegetables to your sandwiches or slice up a slaw!

If you don't like the taste of a raw vegetable, try it steamed, baked or grilled—it will taste different.

REST UP

Sometimes having a busy schedule is fun. It makes you feel important and you get to see a lot of places and a lot of people. But finding a balance is best.

ZZZ!

85 TAKE A BREAK

What counts as a break? A break is when you give yourself some time to relax. You might do something because you want to (not because you have to). Or you might just sit and dream for a little while. Every day needs a balance between feeling busy and feeling relaxed. Here are some ways you can add some quiet time to your day.

Lie down and daydream for 15 minutes.

Write in a journal or doodle quietly.

Read a book in a comfortable chair.

Go for a walk around the block with your family.

86 JUST BREATHE

When was the last time you thought about breathing? It's so automatic that you probably don't even notice you are doing it. But breathing deeply can help you feel calm and relaxed, especially if you are stressed out. When you're nervous or scared, you breathe faster than usual and you may even hold your breath. Try calming yourself down by changing your breathing. Breathe in deeply while counting to three, then breathe out deeply while counting to three. Repeat this a few times until you feel better.

WHOOSH!

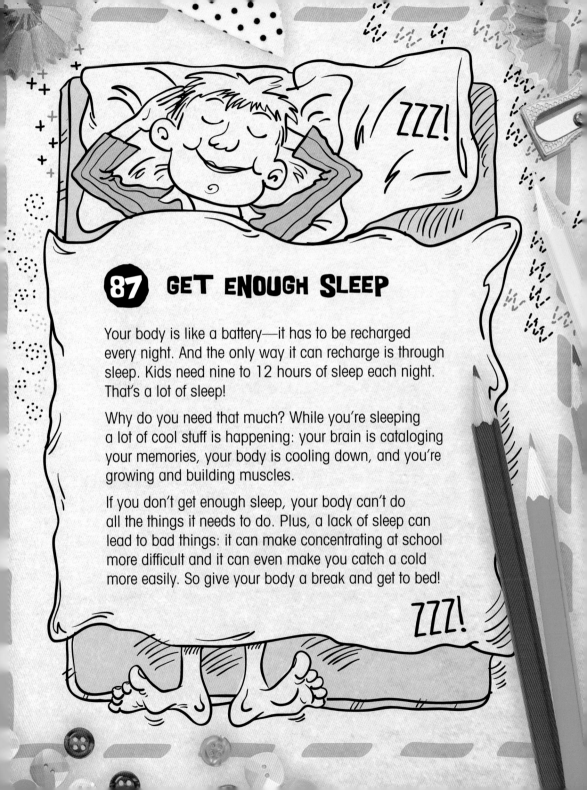

87 GET ENOUGH SLEEP

Your body is like a battery—it has to be recharged every night. And the only way it can recharge is through sleep. Kids need nine to 12 hours of sleep each night. That's a lot of sleep!

Why do you need that much? While you're sleeping a lot of cool stuff is happening: your brain is cataloging your memories, your body is cooling down, and you're growing and building muscles.

If you don't get enough sleep, your body can't do all the things it needs to do. Plus, a lack of sleep can lead to bad things: it can make concentrating at school more difficult and it can even make you catch a cold more easily. So give your body a break and get to bed!

ZZZ!

STAY HEALTHY

Your body needs more than just food and sleep to work properly—it needs you to get moving too!

88 BE ACTIVE

Exercise makes you happier, gives you an energy boost, and helps you sleep better. And those are just a few of the benefits of being active. Amazing, right? You might think that "being active" means exercising or playing a sport. But there are lots of ways to be active. You just have to get moving! Pay attention to how much you are sitting down during the day instead of standing, walking, or playing. Kids should be active for about 60 minutes every day, and it doesn't have to be all at once. Here are some ideas:

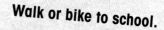

Walk or bike to school.

Do chores around the house or in your yard.

Go for a family walk after dinner.

Stand up while playing a video game instead of sitting down.

Meet friends at a nearby park or playground.

Turn on some music and start dancing!

89 SIGN UP FOR A RUN OR WALK

Get your whole family involved! Organized runs are a really fun way to get active and support a great cause. The entrance fee often goes to a charity or helps bring attention to an important issue.

A 5K is about three miles long and you can choose to walk or run. You can train, which just means you practice running or walking a little bit at a time, together as family, for weeks or months before the main event. When you cross the finish line on the big day, you'll feel like a champion! And tons of people will be cheering you on.

FURTHER READING

Girls on the Run
girlsontherun.org is a club that helps prepare girls for a 5K run.

Let Me Run Boys
letmerun.org is a running club for boys.

Look for nearby races on websites like Running in the U.S.A. **runningintheusa.com**

90 STAY HYDRATED

Did you know that an adult human is made up of about 60% water? Your body needs water to survive, but your body also loses water every day—like when you sweat. The more active you are, the thirstier you get, right?

So while it's important to drink water every day, it's especially important to drink it when you're running around. The water you drink will replace the water you lose. Kids need at least five cups of water per day. And drinking soda or juice doesn't count—sugar and caffeine actually dehydrate your body instead of rehydrating it.

FIND A HOBBY

When you do something you love, it boosts your mood. It can help you relax by taking your mind off anything that may be bothering you, and it gives you a fun challenge.

91 DO SOMETHING YOU LOVE EVERY DAY

What never fails to make you happy? (Your happiness journal from page 87 might help you decide!) Whatever it is, make time to do it every day, even if it's only for five minutes. Consider it "me time."

 listen to music

 play with your little brother

 read before bed

 practice basketball

 take a bubble bath

92 START A BOOK CLUB

Reading is a lifelong pleasure! It's something you can do no matter what age you are—and with so many great books out there, why wouldn't you want to start devouring them now?

Books can teach you how to act in a certain situation, help you deal with problems, and give you a glimpse into someone's life. Plus, you get to travel to faraway places, learn about history, and "meet" new people.

Starting a book club is a fun way to make reading a bigger part of your life. Invite your friends or family members to join, then take turns choosing a book that every member will read. Give everyone about a month to read the book, then meet up to discuss it. You can talk about…

☑ what you liked

☑ what you didn't like

☑ your favorite character

☑ what surprised you

☑ the best part of the book

☑ what you learned

☑ how you think it should have ended

CREATE FAMILY TIME

There's nothing like a family bond. You will always, always be there for each other.

93 SURROUND YOURSELF WITH LOVE

Do photos of family make you smile? Of course they do! Photos can be especially comforting when you're not at home or when a parent or guardian has to travel and you miss them.

Ask an adult to help you print and frame some of your favorite family photos. Place them next to your bed, on your desk, in your locker, in a locket necklace, or on a keychain. Don't forget to include your pets! See? Now you're surrounded by love everywhere you turn.

94 SPEND MORE TIME WITH THOSE YOU LOVE

You don't get to choose your family—but you can choose to love them unconditionally. Get closer to your parents, siblings, extended family members, and anyone else who you consider family. You won't regret it!

Make memories, share stories, and really get to know them. You may not be best friends now, but as you grow older your siblings will become a big part of your life. And you can learn a lot from your parents, grandparents, aunts, and uncles, even if you sometimes disagree with them.

Ask your parents or grandparents to take you to some of their favorite places from their childhood.

Look through photos of your parents or grandparents when they were your age. What were their favorite subjects? What sports did they play?

Start a family tradition, like a Sunday movie night or a Tuesday taco night.

Have a special night out with just you and your mom (or dad) once a month.

Create a secret handshake that only you, your siblings, and parents know.

Start celebrating every family member's half birthday. Make them feel extra special on that day.

CHALLENGE YOURSELF

HMM!

The only way to grow is to push yourself a little bit out of your comfort zone.

HMM!

95 DO A PUZZLE

Mazes, math problems, word searches, whatever! Any kind of puzzle gets the wheels in your head turning and is great exercise for your mental muscles. It's true! Your brain needs exercise just like your body.

QUIZ

What has two hands but cannot clap?

Answer: A clock!

QUIZ

What travels the world but stays in the corner?

Answer: A stamp!

Start a really large puzzle and get the whole family involved.

Create your own word search for a friend to solve.

Pick up a book of crossword puzzles or brain teasers for kids.

Make up a code, by using a symbol for each letter of the alphabet, for example, then write a secret message.

HMM!

96 MEMORIZE SOMETHING

HMM!

Do you feel like your memory isn't that great? Well, maybe you just need some practice.

There are lots of tricks that can help you memorize something, like writing it down, saying it out loud, turning it into a song or a rhyme, imagining pictures instead of words, or creating a mnemonic device.

Pick something—anything—and start memorizing it. It could be:

The eight planets

The alphabet, but backwards

Your favorite poem or song

The notes on the lines of a treble clef

The 50 U.S. states in alphabetical order

QUIZ

Which weighs more—a pound of cotton balls or a pound of bowling balls?

Answer:
Neither. They both weigh a pound!

INFORMATION

WHAT'S A MNEMONIC DEVICE?

It's a trick that helps you memorize something more easily. For example, you could take the first letter of each word to help you remember the order of a series.

My **V**ery **E**ducated **M**other **J**ust **S**erved **U**s **N**achos = **M**ercury **V**enus **E**arth **M**ars **J**upiter **S**aturn **U**ranus **N**eptune.

Now you'll remember the correct order of the planets more easily!

Every Good Boy Does Fine

Use this mnemonic device to remember the notes on the lines of the treble clef!

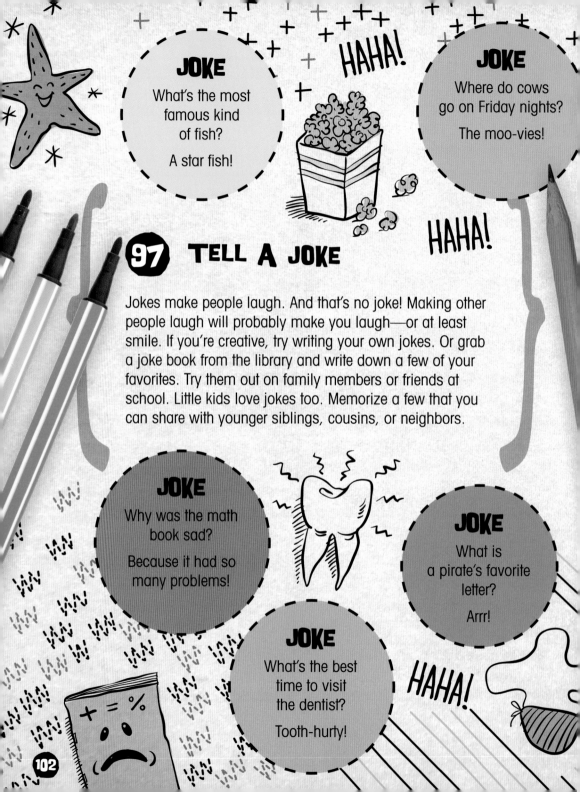

JOKE

What's the most famous kind of fish?

A star fish!

JOKE

Where do cows go on Friday nights?

The moo-vies!

HAHA!

HAHA!

97 TELL A JOKE

Jokes make people laugh. And that's no joke! Making other people laugh will probably make you laugh—or at least smile. If you're creative, try writing your own jokes. Or grab a joke book from the library and write down a few of your favorites. Try them out on family members or friends at school. Little kids love jokes too. Memorize a few that you can share with younger siblings, cousins, or neighbors.

JOKE

Why was the math book sad?

Because it had so many problems!

JOKE

What is a pirate's favorite letter?

Arrr!

JOKE

What's the best time to visit the dentist?

Tooth-hurty!

HAHA!

98 DO SOMETHING THAT MAKES YOU SCARED

You never know until you try. That's how the saying goes! You can probably already think of at least one example when this was true in your life. Sure, stepping out of your comfort zone is scary, but it's also exciting. Instead of being afraid that you'll fail, be proud of yourself for taking a chance.

BEAR TO BE SCARED

If you're scared, think: what's the worst that could really happen? It's probably not nearly as bad as you think!

 Order your lunch at school instead of bringing a lunch.

 Join a club or a sport where you don't know anyone.

 Run for class president.

 Order your own meal at a restaurant.

 Try out for the school play or musical.

 Perform a song or dance in front of your family or friends.

 Stay overnight at someone else's house.

SHARE MORE

Sharing is caring—for others and for yourself.
Because when you share, you feel good!

99 SHARE YOUR TALENTS

What are you especially good at? Playing hockey? Making friends? Solving math problems? Singing? Everyone has a special talent, and you should feel proud yours. Sharing it with others will bring joy into their lives as well as yours.

IF YOU'RE GOOD AT PERFORMING...

Singers, dancers, comedians, and musicians are always welcome entertainment. You could offer to perform for the residents of your local nursing home.

IF YOU'RE REALLY SMART...

Offer to coach a friend or sibling who needs help in a subject you excel at. You could also tutor a younger kid in your neighborhood who is struggling. Ask a teacher or parent to help you set this up.

IF YOU'RE A SOCIAL BUTTERFLY...

Introduce a kid who seems shy or lonely to the people you know. Use your skills to find something that they have in common. Tell them about it during the introduction so they have something to talk about.

100 SHARE YOUR FEELINGS

If you keep all your feelings bottled up inside, you may erupt like a volcano! Sharing your feelings doesn't mean telling your deepest secrets to everyone you know. It means expressing your feelings instead of keeping them hidden inside. Here are some ways you can share your feelings:

Tell your parents when something is making you sad.

If a friend hurts your feelings, tell them why you feel upset.

Talk to a friend or sibling about something in your life that is making you angry or annoying you.

When someone makes you happy, let them know!

LEND AN EAR

If someone else decides to share their thoughts or feelings with you, be sure to listen carefully. Sometimes a friend just needs to know someone cares. You might not even need to say much in return. Just listen.

Keep a journal and write your thoughts in it at the end of each day.

MAKE A SMALL CHANGE

If everyone took one little step it would make a big difference.

101 START A NEW HABIT

Now that you've read this book, it's time to pick one idea that you'd like to try first. That's really all it takes!

Choose something that excites you and that you know you can accomplish with a little effort. Do you want to start with an idea that helps others, helps the planet, or helps yourself? Do you want to choose something small, like turning off the faucet every time you brush your teeth, or something big like starting a club at school? There's no right or wrong answer.

Once you've picked an idea, figure out how you can get started today—not tomorrow, but right now. You may need help or permission from parents, friends, or teachers.

REACH OUT

Get your friends or family involved. The ideas in this book will make a difference, but they'll make a bigger difference when more people participate!

SMALL STEPS

Sometimes tackling a big problem can be overwhelming. Stay positive and don't get discouraged. Just remember: every little bit helps.

STAND TALL

After you've successfully tried one of these ideas, give yourself a pat on the back! You deserve it. Trying your best and setting a good example is what it's all about.

BE HAPPY

If it doesn't work out the way you would have liked, don't worry. Try again or move onto another idea. All you can give is your best.

LOOK FORWARD

Keep at it! Once you've accomplished one idea, try another one. Remember: you may be small, but you can make a big difference!

CHECKLIST

Here's a checklist of all the ideas in the book. Tick each one off when you complete it.

CARING FOR OTHERS

☐ **#1** Smile!
☐ **#2** Talk to a new kid
☐ **#3** Write a thank you note
☐ **#4** Tutor a classmate
☐ **#5** Stand up to a bully
☐ **#6** Spread kindness
☐ **#7** Volunteer your time
☐ **#8** Start a club
☐ **#9** Cheer up a friend
☐ **#10** Share a hug
☐ **#11** Give a compliment
☐ **#12** Celebrate others' successes
☐ **#13** Take on some chores
☐ **#14** Give an award
☐ **#15** Show that you care
☐ **#16** Donate to an animal shelter
☐ **#17** Rescue a pet
☐ **#18** Eat less meat
☐ **#19** Help wildlife thrive
☐ **#20** Donate your old stuff to younger kids
☐ **#21** Donate your ponytail
☐ **#22** Donate sports equipment
☐ **#23** Donate food
☐ **#24** Hold a sale
☐ **#25** Ask for donations instead of gifts

☐ **#26** Donate a portion of your allowance every month
☐ **#27** Volunteer
☐ **#28** Be courteous
☐ **#29** Offer up assistance
☐ **#30** Start a neighborhood library
☐ **#31** Be curious
☐ **#32** Take a CPR or first aid class
☐ **#33** Join a Scouting program

CARING FOR THE PLANET

☐ **#34** Unplug
☐ **#35** Turn off the lights
☐ **#36** Think twice before getting in that car
☐ **#37** Visit a recycling plant or landfill
☐ **#38** Recycle properly
☐ **#39** Pick up litter
☐ **#40** Compost
☐ **#41** Make a homework "mailbox"
☐ **#42** Create a bottle planter
☐ **#43** Design a trinket organizer
☐ **#44** Make an egg carton game
☐ **#45** Say "no" to plastic
☐ **#46** Bring reusable containers to school each day
☐ **#47** Take cloth bags to the grocery store
☐ **#48** Buy used
☐ **#49** Reuse school supplies each year
☐ **#50** Buy local
☐ **#51** Buy things in bulk
☐ **#52** Buy less

- ☐ **#53** Host a swap with your friends
- ☐ **#54** Borrow
- ☐ **#55** Go digital
- ☐ **#56** Use both sides of the paper
- ☐ **#57** Plant a tree
- ☐ **#58** Use fewer paper towels and napkins
- ☐ **#59** Take a shorter shower
- ☐ **#60** Turn off the faucet
- ☐ **#61** Start a mini potted dry garden
- ☐ **#62** Help your family be "green" when doing laundry
- ☐ **#63** Plant a garden
- ☐ **#64** Speak up!
- ☐ **#65** Visit a national park
- ☐ **#66** Educate others

CARING FOR YOURSELF

- ☐ **#67** Be your own biggest fan
- ☐ **#68** Ask for help
- ☐ **#69** Say yes!
- ☐ **#70** Say no!
- ☐ **#71** Don't beat yourself up
- ☐ **#72** Stop comparing yourself with others
- ☐ **#73** Look on the bright side
- ☐ **#74** Love yourself
- ☐ **#75** Stand tall
- ☐ **#76** Don't hold grudges
- ☐ **#77** Get outside
- ☐ **#78** Disconnect
- ☐ **#79** Celebrate the little things
- ☐ **#80** Join a sports team

- ☐ **#81** Make a happiness journal
- ☐ **#82** Eat breakfast
- ☐ **#83** Have a healthy snack
- ☐ **#84** Eat more fruits and veggies
- ☐ **#85** Take a break
- ☐ **#86** Just breathe
- ☐ **#87** Get enough sleep
- ☐ **#88** Be active
- ☐ **#89** Sign up for a run or walk
- ☐ **#90** Stay hydrated
- ☐ **#91** Do something you love every day
- ☐ **#92** Start a book club
- ☐ **#93** Surround yourself with love
- ☐ **#94** Spend more time with those you love
- ☐ **#95** Do a puzzle
- ☐ **#96** Memorize something
- ☐ **#97** Tell a joke
- ☐ **#98** Do something that makes you scared
- ☐ **#99** Share your talents
- ☐ **#100** Share your feelings
- ☐ **#101** Start a new habit

FURTHER READING

All of the following books and websites are aimed at children who are ready to read *101 Small Ways to Change the World.*

KIDS WHO ARE CHANGING THE WORLD
Sourcebooks Jabberwocky (2014)
This book presents 45 young people who are trying to make our planet a better place to be. It also includes suggestions on how you can get involved in championing the planet.

HEROES OF THE ENVIRONMENT: TRUE STORIES OF PEOPLE WHO ARE HELPING TO PROTECT OUR PLANET
Chronicle Books (2009)
This book tells the true stories of 12 very different people who have become environmental heroes by putting their beliefs into action. Its illustrations, photos, and simple language make this title engaging and accessible for all.

WHERE DO GARBAGE TRUCKS GO?
Sterling Children's Books (2016)
Find out what happens to all the rubbish that is created every day. This book is great for helping you understand the consequences of your daily actions and change your habits in pursuit of a better environment.

BACKYARD EXPLORER
Lonely Planet Kids (2017)
Discover a host of ecologically kind activities you can do as soon as you step outside with this interactive book. You complete the pages as you explore your local area so it can become a treasured scrapbook-style journal.

ONE WELL: THE STORY OF WATER ON EARTH
Kids Can Press (2007)
Offering a strong message about our collective responsibility to take care of one of Earth's most precious resources, this book is beautifully illustrated and informative about water sources and conservation.

NATIONAL PARKS GUIDE U.S.A.
National Geographic Kids (2016)
Crammed with photos, maps, facts, activities, and conservation tips, this guide is a must for families that like to hike, as well as those that want to get started.

THE STICK BOOK
Frances Lincoln (2012)
As the title suggests, this book is full of creative ideas for things to do with a stick. It promotes outdoor activities with conservation, adventure, and bushcraft themes.

NO WORRIES!: AN ACTIVITY BOOK FOR YOUNG PEOPLE WHO SOMETIMES FEEL ANXIOUS OR STRESSED
Studio Press (2017)
This activity book is bursting with ideas for combating negative feelings. It aims to help you let go of the things that are worrying you, or work through them if you want to.

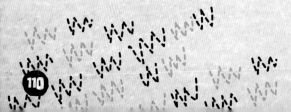